# Adventures in Cartooning
# Christmas Special

James Sturm

Andrew Arnold

Alexis Frederick-Frost

**L**et's start with the boldest of expeditions: climbing Mount Everest in the direst conditions!

As I reached the summit, the blizzard did blast! The cold numbed my body...

How long can I last?!

I thought I'd black out,
but then it all

just

went

white...

When I awoke things were even more dire! Out of the frying pan—into the fire!

I had been captured by the mysterious yeti...

...who tried to eat me like a piece of spaghetti!

I moved lightning fast to thwart his attack: grabbed a bone from the floor and...

WHACK! WHACK! WHACK!

Okay, Mister Yeti, not to be rude, but I **REFUSE** to be your food!

In the land of the giants,
the kids like to play.
They build giant snow-
men and ride giant sleighs.

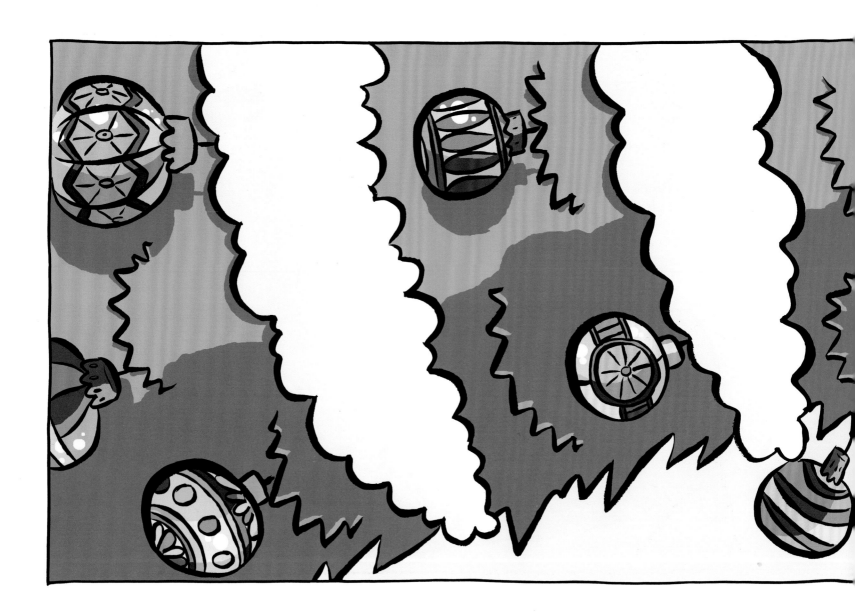

24

But the most <u>impressive</u> thing of all is a Christmas tree **TEN MILES TALL!**

The giant kids' sorrow was too much to face,
so I put on a jet pack and leapt into space!!!

There were SO MANY stars, each one of great worth,

but I picked out the brightest to take down to earth!

On Christmas morning a great miracle was seen— all of the children turned off their screens. They took out some paper and started to draw...

...the things they imagined...

...and things that they saw.

cat

Monsters and heroes were sketched into boxes...

...and robots and rockets...

...and even some foxes!

Or draw a special vacation OR a favorite food!

This will put Santa in a better mood!

Put your comic in an envelope with a stamp for the toll.

Send to this address— it's half way to the North Pole!

RETURN ADDRESS

COMIC FOR SANTA
THE CENTER FOR CARTOON STUDIES
P.O. BOX 125
WHITE RIVER JUNCTION, VT
05001

—Special thanks to Charlotte, Eva, Isabel, and Sage
for contributing some great drawings!

—And thanks to Calista for her rhyme massages,
it was like sending the book to an awesome spa!!!

:01

First Second

New York & London

Published by First Second
First Second is an imprint of Roaring Brook Press, a division of Holtzbrinck Publishing Holdings Limited Partnership
175 Fifth Avenue, New York, New York 10010

Distributed in the United Kingdom by Macmillan Children's Books, a division of Pan Macmillan.

Cataloging-in-Publication Data is on file at the Library of Congress

ISBN: 978-1-59643-730-2

First Second books are available for special promotions and premiums.
For details, contact: Director of Special Markets, Holtzbrinck Publishers.

First edition
2012
Printed in China by South China Printing Co. Ltd., Dongguan City, Guangdong Province

10 9 8 7 6 5 4 3 2 1

# NEW FEATURE: THE TOE KNOWS!

Hey, Toe, this Christmas book is a great stocking stuffer but I have three stockings!

I'm an expert on filling stockings!

Kids (and grown-ups, too!) **LOVE** this book! It teaches the basics of cartooning!

Plus, it's a great story!

The Center for Cartoon Studies Presents:

ADVENTURES in CARTOONING

motion lines

How to turn your doodles into comics!

word balloon

YEAH!

sound effect → GRRRRR

← pencil

by James Sturm, Andrew Arnold, and Alexis Frederick-Frost

The Center for Cartoon Studies Presents

ADVENTURES in CARTOONING

Let's make comics together!

YOU HERE!

COOL!

ACTIVITY BOOK!

by James Sturm, Andrew Arnold, and Alexis Frederick-Frost

In this book, **YOU** get to draw!!

Tons of fun!!!

Toe, can you recommend a stocking stuffer for me, too?

That's a lot of stockings! I may need to look at the First Second catalog for some suggestions!